DREA

The Secret to SUCCESS

Mayooran Senthilmani
ACMA, CGMA, MSc, BSc

Award Winning Author

Foreword by
Raymond Aaron
New York Times Bestselling Author

Disclaimer

This book is designed to provide information and motivation to our
readers. It is sold with the understanding that the author and publisher are
not engaged to render any type of psychological, legal, or any other kind
of professional advice. The content is the sole expression and opinion of
its author. Neither the publisher nor the individual author(s) shall be liable
for any physical, psychological, emotional, financial, or commercial
damages, including, but not limited to, special, incidental, consequential or
other damages. Our views and rights are the same: You are responsible
for your own choices, actions, and results.

Published by DVG STAR Publishing

ISBN: 1912547007
ISBN-13: 978-1912547005

I DEDICATE THIS BOOK TO YOU, THE READERS, TO INSPIRE YOU TO ACHIEVE CONTINUOUS SUCCESS AND MAKE THE WORLD A BETTER PLACE.

CONTENTS

"YOUR LIFE IS A GAME,
YOU ARE THE PLAYER,
SOCIETY IS YOUR AUDIENCE.
USE YOUR MENTOR AS YOUR COACH,
FOLLOW YOUR RELIGION AS YOUR GUIDANCE,
MAKE USE OF OPPORTUNITIES
TO LIVE YOUR LIFE AND INSPIRE THE FUTURE.
YOU ARE THE WINNER,
YOU ARE THE STAR
AND
YOU ARE THE CREATOR OF YOUR OWN
DESTINY."

— **MAYOORAN SENTHILMANI**

ACKNOWLEDGMENTS

Huge thanks to my Mentor, Raymond Aaron (New York Times Best Selling Author, The Nation's Number #1 Success and Investment Coach), for his inspiring words and powerful guidance in publishing my first book.

I would like to take this opportunity to thank my Boss, who inspired, motivated and guided me to progress in my career over the past 10 years to reach my current role as Finance Director.

I am extremely grateful to my lovely wife, Labosshy Mayooran (Author of "Mumpreneurs"). This book would not have been possible without her support and encouragement.

My sincere thanks goes out to....

Dr Marina Nani (Founder of Radio W.O.R.K.S. World Chief Editor, The Quantum of Light and Sovereign) & Philip Chan (10 Seconds Maths Expert, Double Amazon #1 Bestseller) for their continuous support and guidance in my journey

Radio W.O.R.K.S Ltd for my creative book cover design

My Photographer, Olga Solovei, for the fantastic front cover photo of myself

My Editor , Dayna, for the editing of my book

DVG Star Publishing for the publication of my book.

Further thanks go to my brother, Thuvarakan Senthilmani & my friend, Karthik Balachandrarajan, for their assistance in improving this manuscript and to my cousin, Shankar Bavan, for his help in building the website for my book.

My final thanks go to my parents, teachers, relatives and friends, who helped me to reach this level in my life.

Here are some of the people and Institutions that already have a copy of my book.

Her Majesty Queen Elizabeth II

British National Library

Bodleian Libraries (University of Oxford)

Cambridge University Library

Raymond Aaron
(New York Times #1 Bestselling Author)

J T Foxx
(World's #1 Wealth and Business Coach)

Andy Harrington
(The World's Leading Public Speaking Coach)

FOREWORD

Dream Big – The Secret to Success by Mr. Mayooran Senthilmani will guide **YOU** to achieve **SUCCESS** by understanding the basic law of success.

Whether you are a student, employee or business owner, this book will encourage you to find **YOUR** actual passion and then guide you to transform your passion into success. By being truthful with **yourself** and others, **you** will find huge power and success in the current information age, which is one of the most fascinating eras for entrepreneurs.

In this book:

You will explore the current opportunities available to you and how to utilize those opportunities to reach success.

You will start to become more powerful by identifying your real talents.

You will see Where You Are Now! Where You Want To Go In Your Life! How You Can Use **THE A to Z SUCCESS VEHICLE ™** to reach your final destination by dreaming big!

As a final benefit, **Mayooran** has gathered together for you some special bonuses and powerful tools. You can access them effortlessly by simply following the simple instructions in this book.

Raymond Aaron,
New York Times Best Selling Author,
The Nation's Number #1 Success and Investment Coach

~CHAPTER 1~

MY JOURNEY

You may think he is so lucky to have become so successful in life, how did he do it? Trust me when I say hard work and determination pay off. You need to be patient in life, be generous to others, and fortune and blessings will follow. My journey hasn't always been filled with happiness; there have been so many ups and downs, so many struggles I had to face. However, not giving up and believing in myself has brought me to the prestigious status I have achieved today.

I am a Group Finance Director working in London, where I manage £50 million turnover businesses with over 1000 employees.

At present, I am undertaking my doctorate degree in Business Administration at Edinburgh Business School, Heriot-Watt University. I am also a Chartered Global Management Accountant (ACMA, UK), holding an MSc degree in Accounting with Finance and a BSc degree in Mathematics.

I live in England with my loving wife and two adorable children.

A little bit about myself: I was born in Chavakachcheri, a small village in the province of Sri Lanka where having electricity was very rare. My father was a maths lecturer and my mother was a science teacher. My parents were well known by everyone in the village, as our society gives high recognition to education.

"Education is the most powerful weapon which you can use to change the world." - Nelson Mandela

However, in our society, education was used as a weapon to escape the civil war that had been taking place for more than thirty years. Due to the war, every parent wanted their children to be educated so that one day they could pursue their studies abroad to escape the civil war. Most people emigrated to the UK, Australia, Canada and even the USA. My childhood dream was to one day be able to continue my higher studies in the UK.

With my parents' guidance I was one of the brightest children in my peer group. We had a ranking system in school in which everyone competed to be top of the class. I studied in a mixed school and the competition was very high, especially among my friends, because if we ranked top of the class we got to receive our certificates on stage. This positive competition helped me to lay a very strong foundation for my future successes.

Why this burning desire to achieve success?

In 2000, I was studying for my GCSE exam. Suddenly the big war started between the minority LTTE and the government army. Multi-barrel rocket launchers were used by the army to target our village. We all got trapped in the war zone. Our house was destroyed. We lived in bunkers under trees for several days without food. So many people died every day, and many with serious injuries. At that time I was only 16 years old and was distraught to see so many people suffering, injured and even dying right in front of me. During that time I was praying for everyone to be safe. My parents, along with a few of our relatives, decided to try and escape from the war zone to a safe place, mainly to safeguard their children. We had to walk 10 miles, through forests and muddy lands, to reach the safe zone. Even though we were so distraught to be leaving our hometown where we had lived and built our home, there was nothing there for us anymore. We had lost our homes, so we took the chance to escape to reach the safe zone where we knew we would survive and could start thinking about rebuilding our lives. I was saddened by the fact that all we had left of our childhoods was our memories. All my childhood photos, certificates and even my stamp collection were destroyed. That's when I realised that materialistic items are never important; you shouldn't dwell on them. Money will come and go but if you make a legacy of yourself then that will last forever. At that moment I promised myself that I would always achieve everything I set out to do and build a name for myself.

Crossing over to the safe zone, we all carried white flags with us to make sure none of us got attacked as it was a symbol of peace. My father was totally heartbroken after losing houses that he'd built and all his assets that he had worked day and night for. I had to comfort and assure him that money and possessions will come and go, and he should be grateful that he survived despite all that was happening. Over 100,000 innocent people were killed during the civil war in Sri Lanka.

Luckily my parents had some savings in their bank account, which we used to relocate to Colombo, the capital of Sri Lanka. This is where we started from scratch. At the beginning, we lived in a small room which had around ten of us squeezed in together. Those days were the toughest times as I had to pursue my education in a new school and make new friends. All my books had been destroyed and my mother had to ask around and managed to get the books I required for school. Since then, my dream was to pursue my higher studies in the UK.

Every day I studied very hard day and night. I got very good results for my GCSE and A-Levels. I then went to study a maths degree at the University of Colombo.

I am still very proud of Sri Lanka because education is FREE and all medical facilities are FREE. This was introduced by the British when they were ruling the country, and it has remained well after independence in 1948.

However, the university spots are limited and therefore you have to score very high marks to get admitted. I was lucky enough to go to university and complete my first degree for FREE.

While I was at university, I learned how to use the computer and the benefits of the internet. I began to research how to emigrate to the UK. Then I found out that if I could complete the Chartered Management Accountants exams, I could easily go and take my master's degree in the UK with a scholarship, and then if I could find a job I could also settle down there.

I love cricket and chess, which I have played for my school. But at university I decided to sacrifice playing all sports and any extracurricular activities just so that I could complete the CIMA. I went to weekend classes and completed all my CIMA exams whilst doing my BSc degree. At the same time I also gained work experience by working for KPMG, one of the global financial giants.

My dreams came true and I was overwhelmed to have been chosen to start my master's degree in Accounting and Finance in the UK. Thus I emigrated to the UK.

After completing my master's degree, I was eager to find a job in the accounting field. Whilst looking for a job in my field I worked at ASDA as a shop floor assistant. I was granted the work permit by the UK government, allowing me to remain in the UK for 2 years to work. I was determined to find a high paying job in my field to enable me to settle in the UK under the high skilled migration program.

I researched for many nights about how to get an accounting job in the UK. I applied to more than a hundred jobs. All were rejected. I called a few places to inquire about the reason for rejection and their answer was that I didn't have any UK based work experience. So that's when I decided to change my ASDA shift to nights and started to work on a voluntary basis in one of the small accounting firms. After three months I got a paid job as an assistant accountant in central London as maternity cover for nine months. At the end of my contract, I got a permanent job at Caskade Group in 2009 as an accountant and relocated to Bournemouth. I worked hard and developed myself, got promoted to Financial Controller in 2012 and moved to the London office after being promoted to Finance Director in 2014.

Just 10 years ago, I did not know how to get into the accounting field. But now I interview, hire and fire people. I love my job. I always listen to what my heart says and undertake every task with full commitment. This helped me to progress and achieve success in everything I do. In this book, I have written a few useful chapters for you on how to achieve success in interviews (~CHAPTER 12~) and CV writing tips to achieve success (~CHAPTER 13~).

I am so privileged and grateful for everything I have received in my life. I have gone on a very challenging journey to reach where I am today. I hope that my journey will help inspire and motivate you to achieve your own success.
I am very happy with my achievements. But I have always believed that I can do more and I was born to achieve something big.

I listen to motivational talks on YouTube and always keep an open mind. I keep all my doors open to ensure that I don't miss out on any opportunities that come my way.

One day I got an e-mail from Groupon for a ticket to the Entrepreneurs 2012 conference in London where Bill Clinton was one of the key note speakers. I thought maybe it was a sign from God and I should grab this opportunity, so I decided to attend. At the event, I was privileged to meet New York Times bestselling author Raymond Aaron. He inspired me to write a book. But I didn't know where to start at that time.

A year later I met Raymond Aaron again, and under his guidance published my first book, "Live Your Life" in January 2014. The book helped me to improve my personal brand and allowed me to experience several happy moments such as receiving my letter from Her Majesty the Queen.

BUCKINGHAM PALACE

18th February, 2014

Dear Mr Mayooran,

The Queen wishes me to thank you for your letter with which you enclosed a copy of your book, *Live Your Life*.

Your kind thought in sending this publication for Her Majesty to see is greatly appreciated.

I am also to thank you for your message of congratulations on the birth of The Queen's great granddaughter, Mia Grace Tindall, and, once again, for writing as you did.

Yours sincerely

Mary Morrison.

Lady-in-Waiting

The launch of my book opened several doors for me to network with and meet many great and like-minded people. It's not about who you know, it's about who knows you. (I wrote a chapter on how we can increase who knows you, please refer to ~CHAPTER 14~).

My book helped me to increase my visibility and improved my LinkedIn profile. This helped me to increase my connections on LinkedIn from 100 to over 8000 followers. It continues to rise.

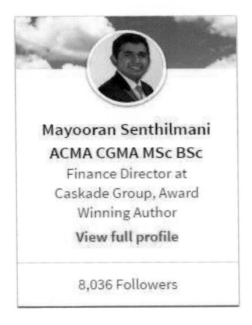

Mayooran Senthilmani
ACMA CGMA MSc BSc
Finance Director at
Caskade Group, Award
Winning Author
View full profile

8,036 Followers

My LinkedIn profile also helped me to get connected with several successful people and I began collaborating with them, working on several projects. From my education and experience, I will show you 'How to use LinkedIn to build your professional brand' in ~CHAPTER 15~.

I also researched and learnt all the techniques required to promote my book, which helped me to take my book to the No. 1 spot on Amazon. Since then I am proud to say that I have helped several other authors to reach Amazon No 1 bestseller status. Helping others to achieve success gives me great motivation and self-fulfilment.

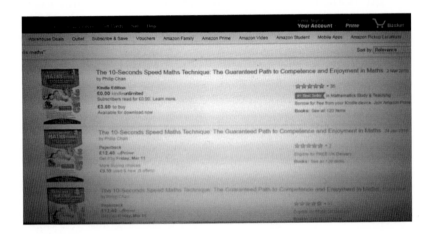

What's next?
I wanted to create something to give back to the world. Thus I have now converted one of my books into a video course for Udemy. Currently, this course has more than 4900 students.

Accounting: Get Hired Without Work Experience
Learn How to Enhance Your Career and Employability Skills
★★★★★ 3.7 (189 ratings)   4,936 students enrolled
Created by Mayooran Senthilmani MSc, BSc, ACMA,CGMA, Universal Learning Academy
Last updated 10/2015   English   English [Auto-generated]

You can access this course on the following link. https://www.udemy.com/accounting-get-hired-without-work-experience/

I would like to give away a coupon code (GIFT) to access my course for FREE just to say thank you for reading my book. This course may not be relevant to you, but it will definitely give you an idea of how you can also create your own online course. This would be another passive income channel for you.

Since 2014 I have written and published the following books: Fire Your Account which I co-authored with my brother Thuvarakan, and Accounting: Get Hired Without Work Experience.

Having published my own books I went on to create my own publishing company to help authors to publish their book in 30 days.

I am the co-founder of Universal Learning Academy, which is FREE online learning platform. This platform currently has more than 100k visitors per month and 20k plus Facebook followers.

The most important take-home message is that education is a necessity, and by dreaming big you achieve great heights!

CHAPTER 2

LIVE YOUR DREAMS, NOT OTHERS'

The industrial age is over. We are living in the digital age, which is also known as the information age. Lots of people are still thinking and living in the industrial age. In the industrial age, people worry about lifetime job security. Even the educational systems of schools and universities were created to fulfil the needs of the industrial age, which were 9 to 5 workers who live their entire lives with the job security to look after their families without looking for more opportunities and without finding their actual ability, capacity and capabilities. This situation is similar to "a frog in the well," where we're not aware of the world outside the well. We all live in our comfort zone. Our parents, school, friends and society influence us a lot and thus we are unable to come out of our comfort zone. In order to do so, we have to exploit new opportunities to inspire the future.

This industrial to information age shift triggered the urgent need of raising more entrepreneurial leaders to solve economic crises. You all need to come out from your comfort zone to see the opportunities. There are plenty of opportunities in the world. This is the wake up call to become an entrepreneur to spot opportunities and act to make them into commercial successes.

In the Dark Age, you were not born to live your life as a slave. But most did.

In the Agricultural Age, you were not born to live your life as a farmer. But most people did.

In the Industrial Age, you were not born to live your life as a factory worker. But most people did.

Now we are in the Information Age. You should not make the same mistakes again and again. You were born to **LIVE YOUR DREAMS** where anything is possible for **YOU**. You can spot the right opportunities and make them successful by living your dreams happily and by inspiring others and the future generation.

You always have to do something you're passionate about. Do something you're good at and do something that makes money. A passionate person attracts opportunities like a magnet.

~CHAPTER 3 ~

DREAM BIG

AND

THINK POSITIVE

It is a true fact that when you are thinking positively you will feel relaxed and more energetic. No long-term success is possible without a positive attitude. This will enable us to develop action plans to achieve our dreams.

One of greatest examples for positive thinking is Michael Jordan, an American former professional basketball player and entrepreneur. MJ was born on February 17, 1963 and is recognized by many people around the world. The National Basketball Association (NBA) website praises MJ as *"By acclamation, the greatest basketball player of all time."*

Michael's **strong determination, rigorous training** and his **attitude** saw him excel in the professional arena where he won many awards and recognitions, such as the most valuable player for five times, and he went on to become a fan favourite. Michael also made impressive comebacks after injuries which at times kept him out of play for months in a row.

Michael also represented his country in the Olympics twice, and in his first Olympic games, he was still a college player.

> *"I play to win, whether during practice or a real game. And I will not let anything get in the way of me and my competitive enthusiasm to win."*

This quote by Michael Jordan shows his passion and commitment to winning.

Michael also emphasizes how a failure needs to be capitalized and learnt from and turned into success. This famous quote by him has inspired many people around the world. *"I've missed more than 9000 shots in my career. I've lost almost 300 games. 26 times, I've been trusted to take the game winning shot and missed. I've failed over and over and over again in my life. And that is why I succeed."*

> *"Some people want it to happen, some wish it would happen, others make it happen."*
> **– Michael Jordan**

How to build positive thinking, a **Six-Step** guide:

1. **Understand that you create your own destiny** – It is always very important for you to understand that you create your own destiny. So it is your responsibility to create your path to success. There are so many people in this world that, when they fail, they put the burden on other people and don't do anything to overcome their failure. You don't want to be one of them. Always have a tight grip on your life. Don't let others control your life.

2. **Make a strong commitment to think positively and not to think negatively** – You can develop these skills by reading books and by reading about

successful people and watching motivational videos, etc. Continuous training and development will enable your mind to think positively even when you are failing.

3. **Be grateful for what you have today** – It is always very important to accept the fact there are so many people in this world having a poorer lifestyle than you. Some people are being treated like slaves and not given any human rights. So utilize your time in an effective way; don't spoil it by thinking negatively. We all are going to be here only once, so make it worthwhile.

4. **Avoid everything that can negatively influence your thinking** – The environment you live in is one of great factors that influence your thinking patterns. There will be people who will always give negative feedback to your approach. It is also a true fact that so many people are so afraid that they don't try to do anything new in their life and are content with living a mediocre lifestyle.

5. **Try humor** – It can be a difficult task to keep a positive attitude when there is little hope for success. No matter how hard life hits you back, it is very important to keep your humor. It will help you to reduce stress and boost your outlook.

6. **Try not to worry; enjoy your life** – There is a strong negative relationship between negative thinking and confidence level. So if we keep on worrying, it is not going to add any value to our life. The only consequence is we may end up making an appointment with the doctor. Trying not to worry is

an art. When you realize that your life is limited, you will start to live your life to its fullest.

You have to surround yourself with highly motivated people and winners. Under any circumstances, you should not allow any negative people to bring you down. You have to find the way to do better and add value to other people and yourself.

~ CHAPTER 4 ~

WORLD LEADERS WITH BIG DREAMS

As a leader, it is always very important to create a positive image about yourself amongst your key stakeholders, including employees, customers, your bank, etc. Learning to think like a confident leader doesn't come naturally. I am going to take the most successful leaders and explain what sort of leadership skills we can learn from them.

Henry Ford
(Ford Motor Company)

"Failure is simply the opportunity to begin again, this time more intelligently. There is no disgrace in honest failure; there is disgrace in fearing to fail"

Henry Ford can be said to be the inventor of assembly line, enabling companies to produce products in mass quantities. He produced the first of many American automobiles that was affordable to the majority of Americans. This assembly-line concept has spread to all mass consumer goods and fast foods, which we enjoy at low cost. He realized his vision of manufacturing an automobile for every American to afford.

Before, forming the company Ford Motor Company, Henry Ford worked as an apprentice machinist, and after that he became an engineer with the Edison Illuminating Company. He committed his awareness to personal experiments on gasoline engines. These experiments resulted in a self- driven vehicle which he called the Ford Quadricycle. Later, he formed the Ford Motor Company, and he built a car known as the Model T, which was cheap at the time. However, Ford needed to present a better motor vehicle. In 1927, successfully launched model A with better technical and engine design. This model sold more than 4 million units. One could say that the driving force for this innovation is captured by one of Henry Ford's sayings:

> *"Enthusiasm is the yeast that makes your hopes shine to the stars. Enthusiasm is the sparkle in your eyes, the swing in your gait. The grip of your hand, the irresistible surge of will and energy to execute your ideas."*

Henry Ford was one of the earliest free enterprise leaders to deduce that paying employees more was essential to retain talent and improve productivity and keep staff morale high. Even though he paid above market rates to employees he managed to manufacture affordable cars. This indicates a shrewd business leader who keeps all stakeholders happy.

His company is still one of the leading car manufacturers in the world.

Warren Buffett

(The most successful investor of the 20th century)

"I always knew I was going to be rich. I don't think I ever doubted it for a minute."

Warren Buffett's path to success is indeed inspiring; hence it is certainly worthwhile learning a bit about this exemplary gentleman.

Warren Buffett is the primary shareholder, chairman, and CEO of Berkshire Hathaway Inc., which is an American multinational company that oversees and manages a number of subsidiary companies.

Buffett was always an enthusiastic financier, even as a child he would work in several part time jobs in order to save up and invest in profitable ventures.
At the tender age of 11, Buffett bought his first stock, investing in 6 shares of Cities Service preferred stock. Over the years, Buffett invested wisely, allowing him to become a millionaire at the age of 32 and subsequently, in 1990, he became a billionaire.

Warren Buffett was determined to become a successful entrepreneur, thus it was his positive attitude which drove him into becoming the exemplary leader he is today.

In spite of Buffett's success, he leads a modest life in comparison to other successful entrepreneurs. He is an avid philanthropist who certainly believes in giving back.

It is his simplicity and determination that drove Warren Buffett to such a successful reign as one the world's most influential people.

Six must-learn lessons from Warren Buffett to achieve success in your life.

1. **On Earning**: "Never depend on single income. Make investment to create a second source."

   You should not depend on one income as this will take a long time to accumulate your wealth and also it will create fear inside you by thinking what will happen if you were to lose that income.

2. **On Spending**: "If you buy things you do not need, soon you will have to sell things you need."

   You have to have discipline. You have to buy only needed items; you should not waste any money on unwanted things.

3. **On Savings**: "Do not save what is left after spending, but spend what is left after saving."

   You have to prepare budget and spend your money. You have to put your savings first before any expenses. Not after.

4. **On Taking Risk**: "Never test the depth of the river with both the feet."

   You should not use all of your resources. You have to be prepared for the worst case scenario of losing everything.

5. **On Investment**: "Do not put all your eggs in one basket."

You have to have a diversified portfolio. That means if you lose one investment, still you will be in the game. Putting all of your money in one type of investment is risky. For example, if you invest all of your money in gold and suddenly the gold price dropped, you will start worrying about your future. The ghost of fear will come into you.

6. **On Expectations**: "Honesty is a very expensive gift. Do not expect it from cheap people."

You have to be honest all the time. But you should not expect it from others. You have to take care of yourself all the time.

Steve Jobs
(Apple)

"Sometimes life will hit you on the head with a brick, but don't lose faith."

Steve Paul Jobs was one of the most prominent and well-known technological entrepreneurs of the modern century. Born on February 24, 1955, Steve was the brain behind the world-renowned company Apple, Inc., of which he was the co-founder, chairman and the CEO. Steve is well known as a creative genius who transformed the lives of many people around the world with the revolution of personal computing through Apple, Inc.

After a power struggle with the board, Steve was fired from his own company in 1985 and went on to establish NeXT. However, Jobs returned to Apple as an advisor years later and eventually became the CEO of the company. Steve brought Apple from near bankruptcy to profitability by 1998.

As the CEO of the company, Steve introduced the iMac, iTunes, iPod, iPhone, and iPad, which have revolutionized how people use mobile devices and computers in the modern era.

As an adopted child, Steve was always interested in electronics from a young age. Upon completing his high school graduation, Steve enrolled in Reed College, which proved to be an expensive college for his parents to afford.

After dropping out of college, Jobs frequently dropped in and out of creative classes such as calligraphy and slept on the floors of dorm rooms of his friends and returned used plastic bottles for cash. Jobs later said, "If I had never dropped in on that single calligraphy course in college, the Mac would have never had multiple typefaces or proportionally spaced fonts." Steve was diagnosed with cancer in 2003 and underwent many treatments, including a liver transplant.

One of Steve's most inspiring quotes is *"Your time is limited, so don't waste it living someone else's life. Don't be trapped by dogma - which is living with the results of other people's thinking. Don't let the noise of others' opinions drown out your own inner voice and most importantly have the courage to follow your heart and intuition."* Steve always encouraged living life based on what makes you happy and not living the lives other people want you to have.

With his never-ending thirst for seeking what he loves to do in life Steve has always been one of the most inspiring people in the modern era.

Richard Branson
(Virgin)

"Never be afraid of weakness, always find a way to convert your weakness into your strength. Experiment with your life and enjoy it to the fullest. Create new paths for your future generations. Screw it, let's do it."

Are leaders made or born? This is an age-old question, one which remains debatable. Whatever makes an individual rise above the rest and set a whole new standard is what gets us all interested in seeking knowledge about such people, in order to determine what inspired them in becoming extraordinary.

Richard Branson is one such individual, who rose above the rest and is still going strong, not only as a successful businessman, but also as a dedicated philanthropist. He is the founder and chairman of Virgin Group.

Losing my Virginity is one of the first autobiographies I read about an exceptional person and one of the books I have always insisted my loved ones should set their eyes upon.

Branson dropped out of school at the age of sixteen; he had a poor academic record as he struggled with dyslexia (Developmental Reading Disorder (DRD)). Being dyslexic never was Branson's downfall; in fact, this was his motivation for becoming the charismatic leader he is today.

Whilst launching campaigns for his many companies, Branson made sure his marketing material would pass on the message the very first time it was launched. This was because being dyslexic guided him in the way he communicated with his customers. Therefore, if he understood the message the first time round and perceived it to be noteworthy, he would go ahead with such marketing material for his campaigns.

This attribute, together with confidence, persistence and determination, made him a successful entrepreneur.

As observers and critics, we could certainly agree that what drove Richard Branson to success was his weakness, as he took his weakness and made it his strength, and the rest is history!

Bill Gates
(Microsoft)

"As we look ahead into the next century, leaders will be those who empower others."

William Henry "Bill" Gates is yet another prominent and well-known technological entrepreneur of the modern century. Born on October 28, 1955, Bill was the co-founder, chairman and the CEO of Microsoft.
Bill Gates is constantly ranked amongst the richest people in the world and has been in the higher ranks for almost two decades.

At the age of 13, Bill enrolled in the Lakeside School where he got the chance to write his first computer program, an application of tic-tac-toe where the user could play games against the computer.

Bill graduated Lakeside School in 1973 and enrolled in Harvard College from which he later dropped out to form a software company along with Paul Allen. This was the beginning of Microsoft.
During his tenure at Microsoft, Bill broadened the company with a range of many products, helping develop the personal computer revolution.

Bill also encourages pursuing life based on what a person loves to do. He also strongly believes in learning from your mistakes. One of his quotes – *"It's fine to celebrate success, but it is more important to heed the lessons of failure"* – emphasizes learning from your failures and mistakes to become a better person.

Bill is a strong believer of books being important to developing his vision and helping him dream and pursue what he loves to do. He said, *"I really had a lot of dreams when I was a kid, and I think a great deal of that grew out of the fact that I had a chance to read a lot."*

Bill Gates is a strong believer in philanthropy. He believes in giving back and has signed up to donate the majority of his wealth to charity. Bill Gates has been an inspiring person to many people, especially with his contributions in the information technology arena.

Mark Zuckerberg
(Facebook)

"I believe that over time, people get remembered for what they build, and if you build something great, people don't care about what someone says about you in a movie… they care about what you build."

Facebook is one of the popular household names in the current era. And the man behind this name is Mark Zuckerberg, who was born in May 14, 1984 and is one of the co-founders, chairman and CEO of Facebook. Mark is recognized as an Internet Entrepreneur as well as an avid philanthropist who has signed up to donate most of his wealth to charity.

Mark launched Facebook from his dorm room in college, and by 2012, he was considered to be a prodigy in computer programming, something he had showed keen interest in since a young age. After enrolling into Harvard, Mark developed Facebook as a networking tool amongst local colleges and then later took it on to other campuses and countrywide.

Mark eventually dropped out of Harvard to continue his project and now is regarded as one of the 100 wealthiest and most influential people in the world by *Time* magazine.

Mark emphasizes finding what you are passionate about and pursuing it. In the following quote, Mark describes on his passions and how they drove him to be who he is today: *"Find that thing you are super passionate about. A lot of founding principles of Facebook are that if people have access to more information and are more connected, it will make the world better; people will have more understanding, more empathy. That's the guiding principle for me. On hard days, I really just step back, and that's the thing that keeps me going."*

Mark is an inspiration to many of the younger generation with his passionate approach on pursuing what he loves. Beginning as a young computer programmer, Mark has emerged as one of the most successful people below 30 years of age.

Based on the above studies, it is very clear that to become a successful person first of all you should have the passion to achieve your goal. Being an entrepreneur or leader is not an easy task. It involves developing more people and delegating the tasks to achieve your goals. In the meantime, you have to keep your stakeholders happy.

When you become a leader, success is all about developing your followers. It's about making the people who work for you smarter, bigger and bolder. Nothing you do anymore as an individual matters except supporting your team members to achieve your goals as a team.

Following your passion, converting your weaknesses into strengths, enjoying your life, and delegation is the art of leadership.

~ CHAPTER 5 ~

WHERE IS YOUR OPPORTUNITY

The economy is dynamic, innovative, and creates the necessary jobs which require a greater number of young people who are willing and able to become entrepreneurs, who will launch and successfully develop their own commercial or social ventures, or who will become innovators in the wider organisations in which they work. You should not blindly follow what is already in practice; everything depends on how creative, innovative, well-educated, and well-informed the market is. There have been several companies who have nailed this and have become successful in testing times. Examples of organisations who have taken advantage of difficult times, relished them, and fought back to succeed by identifying the gaps and opportunities are Foursquare (started in 2009), and Twitter (started in 2006). So what made them succeed? Their education certainly influenced their attitude, skills and moulded the culture for them to act on their feet. This independent thinking, as well the creative desire, paved way to entrepreneurial thinking from a young age. In addition, consider the number of entrepreneurs who act as role models for the youth of today in the form of thought leaders and mentors.

As important as it is to be creative, innovative and look forward towards the future, it is also imperative that we look at the past and assess what has created success, what has worked for people, when and why they made such a move, and how they did it. We should carefully analyse the technological breakthroughs and learn from them, and it goes without saying that it is this practice that sparked a lot of entrepreneurial ideas within the successful businesses we have heard of.

The industrial revolution in the 1700s was due to the industrial units which were powered by heavy machineries, and the invention of trains and ships. And then in the 1870s, Alexander Graham Bell invented the telephone, which enabled us to communicate through voice no matter where we were; this was the seed for a business to operate in multiple locations and still remain connected to their head office. By the 1900s, the travel industry was further boosted by the invention of objects of flight which we fondly call aeroplanes; however, it is another story that these planes were also used for warfare purposes. The factory line (or assembly line) system, which was conceptualised in 1913, made the factory worker's process similar to that of a well-oiled machine. This led the organisations to cater to mass market and achieve economies of scale. The invention of machines did not stop there: by the 1930s, even farming activities were revolutionized with the invention of the combine harvester, giving the farmer more time to focus on other activities. And the invention that first enabled people to learn information within a matter of few hours, the television, was invented. The automobile industry, the pharmaceutical industry, the personal computer, from the old commodore machines to the new sleek tablet PCs, the internet (world wide web), mobile phones, and finally all the technological gadgets that influence and transform our day-to-day life, which in turn resulted in the evolution of our culture, attitudes and beliefs. Google changed the internet and the way of doing business in 1998 by making the whole web searchable. Now by using the search engine, you were able to find anything you want, search about anyone you are interested in, find answers for any question you have, and what's more, you were able to do all this in a matter of seconds. This paved way for many more companies swarming into what we now call the SaaS industry, or in other words virtual business. This has fulfilled the dream of staff and customers being anywhere in the world still being able to do business. Work can be done from home, teams can be spread out worldwide, and no one cares. This ability has resulted in an immense difference between the haves and have-nots in the world, and in the drastic mismatch in the economic prowess of countries. People who have thought ahead of the time and also learnt from the past have motored ahead, while others are still lagging behind. These innovations expanded human intellect, increased the life expectancy in the United States through newly developed medicines, and at the same time kept more than 1 billion people from starving.

Have you stopped to think why this happened? Through forward thinking, people who could afford to buy machines multiplied their wealth and made enormous fortunes. Those who didn't have the means went to the factory floor to become faceless and nameless corporate slaves.

We can blame the industrial revolution, which taught the workers and controlled them by planting the idea that by suffering now, they will be able to reap benefits in the future. Often times, people did accept this idea, dropped their independent ideas, and went on working like machines. Our educational institutes too were tasked with creating obedient workers, not entrepreneurs. Before the industrial revolution, people did not create large businesses, but they had a wild imagination and the dream to experiment, they knew what they wanted to do, and both the customers and the entrepreneurs knew each other by name. There was a spirit of entrepreneurship within each individual.

In the early days of the industrial revolution, not everyone was able to set up a factory, owing to the costs that were involved in establishing such a business. However, in today's terms, a person with a mobile phone, a Facebook page, a laptop, and a decent idea can be a winner. These are businesses which have one owner, one worker, and one beneficiary – and the new breed of entrepreneur have arrived. The UK is known for its high number of home bakers, and each one of them is an example of how they fit into this new breed. Another advantage for these small budding companies is that it makes it easy for them to reinvent themselves, refine themselves, and be agile in decision making, because they are small and it does not take a long time to implement the changes compared to large companies. Almost a decade ago, Nokia, was the most innovative company; however, things changed after they expanded. Now they are struggling to catch up with Apple and Samsung. People will matter again, causes will matter again, and maybe we will see a world that works for a lot more people.

In the Entrepreneur Revolution, your most valued asset is your personal brand and reputation. When somebody googles your name, the first page of results is a perfect indication of how the world sees you.

I would like to stress again, the world has changed, and it will continue to change and evolve. The internet has played a large part in this, and has given new powers to every individual who uses it correctly. An example would be the success of "Gangnam Style" by Psy. Psy was unheard of, and what more, K-Pop was restricted to Korea. But within Psy and his team there was mastery in using social media, and this created the unprecedented success for the song which generated millions of dollars. In similar terms, the internet and its facilities has enabled people to host their own podcasts, video blogs, TV channels, and radio channels, and all these are being used to sell merchandise. All that is necessary is a good idea and a creative way of getting it across, and when I say getting it across, it means globally. People in Asia watch the video channel of 'Super Woman' on YouTube; the views range in the millions, and people spend money buying her merchandise. The evolution of technology allows you to make money from tiny, silly little ideas. Radically, it allows people to make money from their passions.

Of course technology itself is not the answer to the success of ventures; it is part of the reason for the success. While being focused on technology, entrepreneurs also paid enough attention to sales, marketing, product development, management, and business development. This was the result of determination, passion, and drawing inspiration from little successes. This is the simplest of recipes to create and instil an entrepreneur within you. Entrepreneurs know that you have to find a problem, and the solution to that problem will be the product you need to develop. Mere identification won't work, you need to manage the development and see to it that it is accomplished.

When you set up your own business, you have to take some time to carefully think and decide on the following:

a. What type of free gift would you give without expecting any return?
b. How to try out your service without committing to too much money or time.
c. The way to obtain accurate contact information from your potential customers so that they could be offered with your services in the near future, enabling them to be retained

as your permanent customers.

Then your core product can deliver a full solution to what people want and seriously solve problems.

You should always under-promise and over-deliver. If you focus on creating success for your clients, they will go out and tell the world.

~ CHAPTER 6 ~

THE POWERFUL FORMULA FOR SUCCESS

DREAM -> VISION -> GOAL => SUCCESS

THE POWER OF DREAMS

> *"If you can dream it, you can do it."*
> **– Walt Disney**

Walt Disney

The creator of the international cultural icon Mickey Mouse, Walt Disney started the Disney Empire with great determination and guts. At the age of 22, Walt went into bankruptcy after the failure of a cartoon series. He went to Los Angeles with $40 in cash and a few clothes. Walt and his brother then set up a nascent animation business in California.

Inexperienced in business, Walt had to face problems of the ownership of his animated characters. He realized that the ownership of the animated cartoon character Oswald the Lucky was with the distributor. The power the distributor had over Walt and his other artists eventually led him to relinquish the business and start one on his own again.

Walt Disney was once quoted as saying, *"As long as there is imagination left in the world, Disneyland will never be complete."* Although Disney theme parks were not yet built at the time, Walt Disney's imagination led him to start another character, Mickey Mouse, with his old and loyal friend. This iconic Mickey Mouse character had many infectious and enjoyable traits such as his energetic and enjoyable personality, entertaining actions and most important of all, laughter.

Walt Disney said that *"Laughter is America's most important export."* Walt Disney identified that he needed to create new character to satisfy a growing nation's appetite for humour.

Today, after his death, the Disney Empire is still going strong.

THE POWER OF VISION

Learn the power of VISION from Abraham Lincoln

Abraham Lincoln's VISIONARY leadership abolished slavery in the United States. Abraham Lincoln was the 16th president of the United States of America, as which he served from March 1861 until his assassination in April 1865. His determination to end slavery was finally recognized in 1865 by which salves were freed in nationwide.

Being regarded as one of the Americas greatest heroes, Lincoln possessed a unique appeal which had an incredible impact on the nation; he used such traits to bring about the best in the United States.

His rise to being the 16th president of the United States was from a humble beginning. His beloved mother died at the age of 34 when Abraham was just 9 years old, this alienated him from his father even more with whom he did not bond well. His father remarried, but unlike typical step mothers Sarah bonded well with Abraham, it was she who encouraged Abraham to read. Abraham received his formal education whilst growing into his manhood, an estimation of 18 months in total. He was mostly self-educated; in fact, he educated himself in becoming a successful lawyer.

His political career began in 1832 by which he ran for a seat in the Illinois House of Representatives, but he lost the election. He ran again in 1834, and won; he served in the Illinois House of Representatives until 1842.

Abraham Lincoln was elected president on 6th November 1860 and assumed office on 4th March 1861. He was re-elected on 8th November 1864 and served until his assassination on 15th April 1865.

Lincoln was a determined man not only to succeed for himself but also for the country he loved so much.

> *"Always bear in mind that your own resolution to succeed is more important than any one thing."*
> **-Abraham Lincoln**

THE POWER OF GOALS

The Power of **GOALS** is explained in Chapter 10 under the application of the *A to Z SUCCESS MODEL* ™ for your success journey.

Setting goals and achieving them is a vital part of success. But this is not a goal setting book, so I can't go into more detail on how to set or achieve goals.

However, my mentor and friend Raymond Aaron has written a best-selling hardcover book, *Double Your Income Doing What You Love*. Raymond is recognised as the world's # 1 authority on goal achievement.

In fact, on the back cover, there are testimonials from giant celebrities who use his program. One such testimonial is by Jack Canfield, the co-creator of the *Chicken Soup For The Soul* series of books.

Here is his testimonial: *"The reason I personally chose to use this amazing system for myself and for my company is that, bluntly stated, it is the most powerful system ever created."*

By special arrangement, I have permission to allow you, my dear reader, to own a copy of Mr Aaron's book for free and you can get it by instant download simply by going to his website. www.aaron.com.

~ CHAPTER 7 ~

HOW TO OVERCOME PROCRASTINATION

> *"Procrastination is the bad habit of putting off until the day after tomorrow what should have been done the day before yesterday."*
> **- Napoleon Hill**

Procrastination permits your mind and body to switch off from being productive. Procrastination will reduce your self-esteem and also will lower your reputation in the eyes of others. This needs to be solved with immediate effect by making sure you take necessary action.

Six Action Plan Guides to Overcoming Procrastination:

1. Just start!

You have to start first. No point in talking. You have to take action now. If you are planning to start a business, start today! Start now! Once you have started a task, you will feel great about yourself, which will drive you forward towards success. You have to create a to-do list and organise your time to get your entire task done as per your schedule.

Once you gain momentum, you will become more productive and thus beating the battle against procrastination.

2. Take Breaks and Think about the Next Step

This will help you immensely to eliminate procrastination. Taking short breaks, for just, say, 15 minutes after working for a solid period of time, will refresh your thoughts and prevent your mind from wandering. You could take short refreshing breaks, do some light exercise, practice some breathing techniques, or even meditation will allow you to work more efficiently and to stay more productive to finish your task rather than procrastinating. However, technological distractions should be minimised for your short breaks to be effective.

3. Be Motivated

You should always list the most important tasks first on your list to try and avoid temptation of leaving them till the last minute. By ticking of the most important tasks first will give you self-accomplishment and motivation. This motivation will give you the willingness to complete the rest of the minor things pending on your list.

4. Keep Commitments Under Control

You should try and avoid committing to too many things. Prioritise your time enabling you to have some time for relaxation for both your mind and body. By keeping your commitments under control you are less likely to procrastinate as there will be fewer tasks to focus on and people will take less advantage you by piling on more and more work for you to do, thinking that you will be able to cope.

5. Delegate Your Tasks

You have to learn to delegate your task to the right people and provide clear instructions and guidance for them. You have to give clear instructions during the delegation and also monitor the progress. This will help you to reach long term success.

This will allow you with some extra time to concentrate on key tasks and also to focus on how to drive your business forward.

6. Improve Your Decision Making and Time Management Skills.

If you want to get your task done, either you have to have the sound time management skills to finish all tasks on time or you have to take the decision to delegate it to someone to get that job done. Therefore, both decision making skills and time management skills are essential to overcoming procrastination.

~ CHAPTER 8 ~

IDENTIFY AND OVERCOME FEARS

A state of mind is something that one assumes. It is not something that can be purchased, but something that has to be created. The "fears" are sufficient enough to destroy your chances of achieving a high standard in any undertaking. They will wipe out your passion and make self-control impossible, lead to indecision, discourage creativity and encourage procrastination.

By far, the most transformational book that I have read to date is Think and Grow Rich by Napoleon Hill. This book helped me to drive fear and negative thoughts away from my life. I would like to take this opportunity to guide YOU on how to overcome YOUR FEARS with what I have learnt from the teachings of Napoleon Hill.

FEAR NUMER ONE: THE FEAR OF POVERTY

The fear of poverty is ruining most of our successes. Most people who are working for a company try to buy a car through a loan and a house through a mortgage. The current economic climate triggered people to worry about losing their jobs. This automatically will develop into worrying about paying off mortgages and how to survive on a day to day basis. Because of this, most people seek job security for their lifetime rather than finding new opportunities to make a fortune in the future.

Are you suffering from this fear?
Please answer the following to get your answer:

a.   Do you lack ambition?
b.   Are you ready to tolerate poverty?
c.   Are you ready to accept any kind of compensation life may offer without objection?
d.   Are you feeling mentally and physically lazy?
e.   Do you lack initiative, creativity, passion and self-control?

If you answered Yes, YOU ARE affected by this **FEAR**.

Now jot down the number of Yeses you collated from this type of fear. Do this for each fear hereafter. This will be discussed later within this chapter to identify the ways to overcome the effect of fear on YOU.

FEAR NUMER TWO: THE FEAR OF CRITISCISM

Fear of criticism will kill your initiative, destroy your creativity, take away your independence, restrict your individuality and will do you damage in several other ways.

For example, irreparable injury could be caused to a child by their parents who unknowingly criticise them if they don't achieve a high grade in school. This can result in rebelling against them, dropping out of school, and ultimately walking a path of fear.

Are you suffering from this fear?
Please answer the following to get your answer:

a. Are you self-conscious?
b. Do you lack self-confidence?
c. Do you have an inferiority complex?
d. Do you lack initiative and ambition?
e. Do you lack personality?

If you answered Yes, **YOU ARE** affected by this **FEAR**.

FEAR NUMER THREE: THE FEAR OF ILL HEALTH

The human mind builds and destroys. It is very powerful in a sense that visuals have been inserted into your mind to question what would happen when you die due to ill health.

Are you suffering from this fear?
Please answer the following to get your answer:

a. Are you a hypochondriac?
b. Do you have the habit of using alcohol or cigarettes to destroy any kind of pains?
c. Are you thinking about imaginary illnesses?
d. Do you avoid outdoor life and reluctant to do exercise which resulted in you being overweight?
e. Do you have a habit of reading about illnesses or reading medical advertisements?

If you answered Yes, **YOU ARE** affected by this **FEAR**.

FEAR NUMER FOUR: THE FEAR OF LOSS OF LOVE

This fear will be the one that will hurt you the most out all of the six fears. Your body and mind are summoned to this fear, which may lead you to insanity. It will play with your emotions and get in the way of success by blinding you from seeing the truth in front of you.

Are you suffering from this fear?
Please answer the following to get your answer:

a.   Do you have the tendency of being suspicious without rational evidence?
b.   Do you have the habit of finding fault with others?
c.   Do you have the habit of gambling to provide for your loved ones?
d.   Do you have the habit of spending beyond your limit to provide a gift for your loved one?
e.   Do you have a lack of determination, self-discipline, self-confidence and less willpower?

If you answered Yes, **YOU ARE** affected by this **FEAR**.

FEAR NUMER FIVE: THE FEAR OF OLD AGE

The anxiety of old age is a result of this fifth fear, triggered by the likelihood of illness, hardship, loss of freedom and independence.

Are you suffering from this fear?
Please answer the following to get your answer:

a.   Do you have an inferiority complex?
b.   Do you have the habit of killing your initiative?
c.   Do you lack imagination?
d.   Do you have the habit of talking about being old?
e.   Do have the habit of dressing with the aim of trying to appear much younger?

If you answered Yes, **YOU ARE** affected by this **FEAR**.

FEAR NUMER SIX: THE FEAR OF DEATH

In truth we all fear death, even though none of us knows what awaits us in the afterlife. Heaven and hell are mere illusions of our imagination; neither you nor I know whether either world exists. This fear is useless. Death will come no matter how we try to prevent it. It is unavoidable, so you should put the thought out of your mind.

Are you suffering from this fear?
Please answer the following to get your answer:

a. Do you constantly worry about dying instead of living your life?
b. Do you feel as though you don't have any purpose to live?
c. Do you worry about ill health?
d. Do you worry about poverty?
e. Do you suffer from disappointment over love?

If you answered Yes, **YOU ARE** affected by this **fear**

If you get all five Yeses in each of these fears, **YOU ARE HEAVILY** affected by this fear and you have to take immediate action. If you get zero, you are **NOT** affected by this fear, so no need to worry. Please use the table below to collate your answers.

YOUR FEARS	YOUR SCORE
NUMBER 1: **POVERTY**	
NUMBER 2: **CRITISCISM**	
NUMBER 3: **ILL HEALTH**	
NUMBER 4: **LOSS OF LOVE**	
NUMBER 5: **OLD AGE**	
NUMBER 6: **DEATH**	

To overcome these fears you have to be able to prevent yourself from being jealous of others, avoid being greedy, believing in superstition, getting angry for no reason and avoid hatred and the desire for revenge. By doing this you are one step closer to overcoming your fear.

The greatest remedy for fear is CREATING A BURNING DESIRE to achieve your goals and provide useful service to others.

I would personally recommend you to read Napoleon Hill, *Think and Grow Rich (1938)*, to learn more about overcoming fears and achieving success.

~ CHAPTER 9 ~

HOW TO TURN DEFEAT INTO VICTORY

Defeat, most of us are afraid to face. Sometimes we don't try anything new mainly due to fear of failure. Fear of failure is one of greatest negative factors which can make a person think that he cannot do anything in his life. I have a friend who was a very intelligent chap in our school. After leaving school, he was the first person to get a job in a leading firm. We were really proud of him. Life moved on, and after three years I met him. I asked him how he was. He replied, *"Horrible, man."* He continued, *"I am unable to complete my undergraduate degree. I cannot study. I have failed so many times. Now I quit my job also. I'm not going anywhere."* I asked him how he was financing himself. He replied in a low voice, *"My mother is providing for me again."*

It is always important to stay focused during the hard times. Everyone fails in their life. It is all about how you fight back.

> *"I never thought of losing, but now that it's happened, the only thing is to do it right. That's my obligation to all the people who believe in me. We all have to take defeats in life."*
> **–Muhammad Ali**

Ali was a normal African American guy who, by realizing his gift of speed, achieved great success. He never feared any of the obstacles that came his way in the form of racism, and became stronger in spirit with every problem faced in his life.

Ali became heavyweight champion of the world after beating Sunny Liston in 1964.

At the peak of his boxing career Ali had to face the Vietnam War draft, and Ali refused to go. Due to this, Ali was stripped of his boxing title and license and could not fight for nearly two years.

After his return in 1970, Ali, still undefeated, had to face all-conquering Joe Frazier, also known as "Smoking Joe." The bout went on for 15 bloody and gruesome rounds and Joe Frazier was declared the winner. Ali was in his early thirties and had difficulty facing superior punching and speed of younger boxers. However, Ali was asked to fight recently-crowned heavyweight champion George Foreman, who had convincingly beat Joe Frazier to regain the title. All the people were in favor of George Foreman; they said he could beat Ali with ease.

However, Muhammad Ali adopted a successful strategy, the "Rope-A-Dope," where he made his opponent throw punches while Ali leaned on the ropes. George foreman's punches rarely hit Ali. This method made George Foreman expend all his energy and tire. Ali then sensed his time to retaliate and sent down a flurry of punches to knock down the unconquerable and superior George Foreman.

This proves why Ali is still considered the greatest, because he had to fight the best of the best in his era. It's not about losing; it's all about how you come back.

Six Steps to Turn Defeat into Victory

1. **Study your own failure to overcome failure** - There is a famous quote by Thomas A. Edison: *"I have not failed. I've just found 10,000 ways that won't work."* It is a fact that so many people fail miserably and give up their passion very easily with the first defeat. It is all about you identifying the reason for your failure and developing strategies to overcome those temporary defeats.

2. **Have the courage to be your own constructive critic** – You cannot find a better friend than yourself. If we look at the most successful people, they know their weaknesses. For example if we take Sir Alan Sugar, he said, *"I am gambler. I take high risks. Sometimes I get high rewards, sometimes I fail miserably."* So he consults with his high calibre, top-level management before investing in risky projects. However, the final decision is made by Sir Alan Sugar.

3. **Believe in your ideas** – It's really useful to get other peoples' opinions about your failures. The answer can provide a different perspective. However, it is very important that you believe in your ideas and also make sure third parties' negative feedback doesn't sink you very deeply into failure.

4. **Stop blaming luck**
   You have to study each of your defeats to find out what went wrong, how it went wrong, and why it went wrong to prevent repetition in the future by taking necessary steps immediately. You have to remember that blaming luck never got anyone where they wanted to go.

5. Blend persistence with experimentation
You have to be very proactive and think about the outcome well in advance. Stay with your goal; try new approaches and experiment.

6. See the good side
You have to remember that there is a good side to every situation. You have to find it, see the good side, and overcome discouragement.

~ CHAPTER 10 ~

INCREASE YOUR MIND POWER THROUGH SPIRITUAL ENERGY & A HEALTHY LIFE STYLE

Earth's population has surpassed 7 billion as I write this chapter, with an overall life expectancy of 69.92 years. There are more than 190 countries on earth, including the newly formed South Sudan. Each country and its people have different culture and different beliefs, they look different, they talk differently, they work differently; in short, they come from very diverse backgrounds. But, as many gurus have noted in the past, there is a common aspect in each and every one of us, and this is true irrespective of our religion, our language, our faith, our gender, our financial and social status, our aspirations, and our beliefs. That common aspect is that as human beings, all of us want to be HAPPY. But, if we consider if we have all been successful in achieving this, I must say NO, we have made a mistake in this regard. More often than not, we have been wasting a lot of time looking for this happiness in the external environment, whereas it would have been the best choice to spend that time to tap into the bliss within. Heraclitus quoted, "The Only Thing That Is Constant Is Change," which will stand forever. The environment around us will keep on changing, and it is our mistake if we keep expecting to find happiness from the world around us. We should adopt and prepare ourselves to find permanent happiness, and for this we must realise that it is in the soul within that we must invest in to experience eternal happiness.

It is a rough stone that, when identified and uncovered by humans, goes through the process of cutting and polishing before we have in our hands the most precious of stones in the world: the diamond. Before it undergoes that process, it resembles just another stone. Similarly each individual has a bright light of enlightening within us, but it is covered with blankets of worldly needs and is hidden from us. It is this state that makes it difficult for us to find the true state of bliss, and paves the way to spiritual ignorance. Due to this, our mind does not look beyond the five senses. So how have a few people been able to find the bliss within them? This is where meditation, yoga, and recreational activities can help. These are activities that stimulate the search within yourself, where you spend quality time alone, exploring your thoughts, and defining yourself. The practicing of spirituality leads to permanent personality changes, whereby the individual becomes positive in their approach; there will always be a calm approach to every situation (no matter how demanding the situation is), the aura and charisma become infectious, and soon people will want the individual to be their role model and mentor.

Gautama Buddha was a spiritual leader; his teachings laid the foundation for modern day Buddhism. Buddha lived a good portion of his early life in luxury, and once he ventured outside the palace walls, he saw the troubles which will eventually consume all human beings: suffering. To find solutions to the human condition, he initially lived a purely ascetic lifestyle, one in which he did not seek any material comfort or luxury. This lifestyle did not give him mental comfort; this extreme asceticism didn't work. Therefore, Buddha came to the conclusion that one has to live life the "middle way." This meant not too much materialistic comfort and not too much severe asceticism.

> *"All that we are is the result of what we have thought. The mind is everything. What we think, we become."*
> **– Buddha**

So what does Buddhism teach us? What does Buddha's life teach the leaders of today? What should be the summary to take away? Buddhism was conceptualised by Buddha with the aim of teaching a balanced life for humankind. The major reason was to create a practice that promises a peaceful and balanced life. Buddha did not preach it without any practice, he did walk the talk. He had first-hand experience in this approach before he started preaching it to his disciples and asked them to adhere to it. The take away here for the leaders is that they have to lead by example before they implement a plan, model, or any change. Leaders have to master their craft before asking others to follow, and this is the difference between a leader and a manager. Understanding and analysing one's environment increases the success rate of one's ability to direct his troops to execute a plan or idea.

If you practice and gain spiritual energy, you will become as a spiritual leader, giving you the following six benefits which will drive you to success.

1. You will be able to help others make their own connection with the God they believe in

A manager training his employee is similar to a spiritual leader training his disciples. While the problem in hand may be different, the approach they should take up is the approach of enlightenment through questioning themselves and the process. This brings more clarity and makes understanding the process easy.

2. You will be able to lead others to find their own reason and identity

Workplace issues and strategic development becomes the tool to help followers discover their own personality and overcome obstacles standing in their way. By leading employees to function in areas in which they are strong will always be more productive than those who are simply trying to fill a position or role.

3. You will be able to transform others

A charismatic leader will be able to help their followers rediscover themselves, and help them redefine their priorities. This will pave way to loyalty, boosting morale, and higher efficiency on the job. Spiritual leadership will create passion within the followers and transform the powers within.

4. You can create an impact on the environment

When there is worry, fear, or indifference, a spiritual leader can transform the immediate power of these storms and restore vision, energy and hope. A spiritual leader can reduce the hostility of a situation and create a peaceful environment, he will be able to reduce hate and create love, can bring a sense of patience within his team members, treats everyone with kindness which will inspire his or her team morale, and works towards the greater goodness of the business as well as the individuals without cutting corners.

5. You can make people see old things with a different point of view

People have born and bred in a certain culture, and their thoughts dwell on the beliefs they were brought up with. Changing the way they think will do a lot of good in making business and life decisions, as they will be able to evaluate things from more than one view point.

6. You will gain followers because of who you are, not because of a position you hold

Leaders with spiritual beliefs give their employees more to think about and improvise on their own, rather than make them follow instructions. They lead by example, and followers start to follow them because they are inspired by their actions. A good example is Nelson Mandela, who is looked upon as a great leader by both Afrikaners as well as native blacks of South Africa.

A HEALTHY LIFESTYLE

Healthy lifestyle is very important to keep your mind active and powerful, which is essential to your success.

Six Steps to a Healthy Lifestyle

1. Healthy Eating

Maintain healthy eating habits and avoid eating fast food.

2. Maintaining Physical Fitness

Work out and try to maintain fitness through exercising. This lowers the risk of cholesterol and sugar levels.

3. Control Your Diet to avoid Blood Sugar

High blood sugar levels often are the leading cause of diabetes, and it has commonly resulted in blindness and other complications when treating other illnesses such as kidney diseases and nerve damage.

4. Control Your Diet to Maintain Healthy Blood Pressure Levels

Maintaining healthy blood pressure levels ensures that the body receives the needed blood at the correct speed and time. By maintaining a good green diet, the pressure levels are maintained.

5. Control Your Diet to Maintain Healthy Cholesterol Levels

It has been identified that high cholesterol levels have led to the hardening of arteries, which results in slow down of blood, and continuous ignorance will lead to permanent blockage, and hence, a heart attack.

6. Healthy Dieting

A lot of vegetables, fruits, and dairy products taken in a measured way enable us to be healthy. It was the correct mix of these natural products with herbs and spices that kept our ancestors living for a long period, before these so-called advanced medicines were created.

As mentioned in my earlier chapter, changes in the environment have been unpredictable, we have been hit by a recession, and markets have crashed, leading to a rise in unemployment rates. And it must be noted that certain businesses did thrive in this environment, which is an example why you must invest in yourself and empower yourself to be a force to be reckoned with. This book will act as a personal guide to help you assess *where you are now, where you want to get to or want to be, what the gap is, and how you can get there through perseverance and investing in yourself.* You deserve to have more of what you want out of life.

~ CHAPTER 11 ~

TRANSFORM YOUR PASSION INTO PROFIT

BY USING THE

A to Z

SUCCESS MODEL ™

Turning your passion into profit is something that everyone can do. But not everyone has the determination or will power to make it happen. Are you willing to take massive action? Willing to take steps every single day towards achieving your goals? Have role models. Do what successful people have done to become successful. Destroy your obstacles and master your fears.

1) **Identify your passion.** What you enjoy most? You have to enjoy what you are doing to achieve long-term success. This will give you personal satisfaction, financial gain, enjoyment and stability. You have to truly believe in yourself and you have to do it with full commitment.

2) **Set your goals**. You have to set your long-term, medium-term and short-term goals, then create an action plan to reach those goals by creating step-by-step, measurable stages.

3) **Identify your strengths and weaknesses.** You have to develop a winning attitude and have to be very open-minded person, which will help you to spot opportunities and also to turn your failures into successes.

Failure is the first step to success. However, you have to learn from your mistakes and you should educate yourself to make sure that the same mistakes will not be repeated in the future. You have to always be positive to turn your weakness into strengths. **You have to plan everything. A failure to plan means you are planning to fail.** You have to analyse each business opportunities by researching the complete data with an open mind.
Be good at what your business does.

4) **Invest in yourself.** Education is an on-going process. You have to attend business seminars, workshops, and training courses. You have to read business books, magazines, reports, journals, newsletters, websites and industry publications. You have to always think of innovative ways to do things better in less time with less effort. You have to educate yourself with essential skills, such as managing your cash flow. The lifeblood of any business is cash flow. Customers are king; your business is all about your customers. You have to understand your customers and provide personalized attention to gain repeat business. You have to focus on marketing, advertising, and promotional activities to reach your customers.

How can you make a positive and memorable impression on people with whom you intend to do business? Make sure you're keeping up with the high-tech world as it suits your needs. You have to **become known as an expert in your field. You may have to write a book on your field of expertise and publish it, so you will be known as an expert. This will help you build your reputation.** Don't waste time, energy and money. Always focus on improving your business, stimulating ideas, sharing ideas, listening to others, talking about the project, and working with collaborators.

5) **Build a mastermind group.** You have to understand that no one can build a successful business alone. You have to understand that time is key. You need to have more time to drive your business forward. So you have to delegate your task to someone to do it for money. You have to think like a business leader. Let's say you are currently employed and planning to start a business. You should not straight away quit your job and start your business. You have to plan everything first. How your business will function in the future? You have to do your forecast first. How will your business grow in 6 months, 1 year, 2 years, and 5 years? Then you will start working on your own time to develop your business. At one point you will start feeling that you can delegate one task to other person for a price so you can use that time to concentrate more to develop your business further. No one can build a successful business alone. You and your mastermind team will focus to **create a competitive advantage.** Why you, instead of your competitors? You have to hire passionate people and share your passion with them. Keep the passion alive always.

6) **Always aim for success, and take your people with you.**
You have to make sure that you reach maximum personal performance and productivity. You have to have knowledgeable about your products and services. You must be able to provide customers with what they want, when they want it. You have to sell the benefits associated with owning your products and services. You have to help local charities. Get involved in the community that supports your business. And also get involved in

organizing community events. You have to master the art of negotiation. Negotiation is not about who wins. It's about how to reach a win-win situation for a long-term profitable relationship.

7) **Stay organized.** It's about having systems in place to do things. It's about managing your business. Creating a to-do list at the end of each business day keeps you on top of important tasks to tackle. Ensure that jobs are completed on schedule. Create the schedule by considering other commitments. Have the ability to multitask and also be good at delegating tasks to others. You have to put the right people in the right place and at the right time to achieve success.

A to Z
Success Model™

Authority	**N**iche Market
Beliefs	**O**pportunities
Change	**P**ersistence
Dreams	**Q**uality
Education	**R**esult
Failure	**S**acrifice
Goals	**T**ime
History	**U**nderstanding
Innovation	**V**ision
Jealousy	**W**in-Win Situation
Knowledge	**X**-Efficiency
Leadership	**Y**ou
Mind power	**Z**ero-based budgeting

A to Z SUCCESS MODEL ™

A- Authority is your power

Do you have authority? Who is going to give that to you? The answer is no one. You have to find the way to establish authority in your field. For example, if you are a mathematician, you can get a PhD to gain that authority.

However, if you want to have authority in your niche market, the one and only, most effective way is to write a book. For example, if you are a plumber, you can write about selected plumbing techniques you can help with. If you are an electrician, you can write about your own speciality.

We are living in the DIGITAL world. The technique of handing out business cards is outdated. You have to find the way to differentiate yourself. You could to write a book and publish it. It would give you the authority automatically.

Turn your passion into a mission to educate others. Find your unique way to gain authority in your niche.

B- <u>Beliefs</u> *make your reality*

Never give up on your dreams and beliefs as you will never know how worthy you are until you actually put them into action. Self-respect is the key to believing in yourself which will lead you to success.

> *"Working hard is important, but there is something that matters even more: Believe in yourself."*
> — **Harry Potter**

You have to be in control by setting goals for yourself. This will enable you to build on your self-confidence. To become successful you must have realistic expectations.

By comparing the gap between where you are now and where you want to be in the future, you can judge your level of success. This will help you determine what remains to be done. You can also judge by looking at the progress you've made in the past few years to merely a month ago. This will enable you to acknowledge how far you have come.

You should never let others to tell you that you are any less than who you really are. There are some who are judgmental, who get pleasure in putting you down to make them appear bigger and better. However, there are few people who are willing to help you improve through the kindness of their hearts. By focusing on those few people you will be surrounded by positive vibrancy and this will help you to build on your self-confidence, leading to the path of belief.

If you believe you can do it, you can! If you believe you can't do it, you can't! Self-belief is the key to success.

C- Change for Credibility – *You need to focus on the needs and wants of the people. You have to be the change rather than trying to change the world.*

"Be the change that you wish to see in the world."
– Mahatma Gandhi.

In other words, change has to start within ourselves; we cannot expect the world to change if we do not. Instead of focusing on problems, we can start to live solutions.

"Change will not come if we wait for some other person or some other time. We are the ones we've been waiting for. We are the change that we seek."
– Barack Obama

Help, guidance and support are three essential needs for kindness to become a natural expression of who we are. Meditation is one of the forms which can help to achieve this. The more deeply we discover about ourselves, we will begin to realise that we are more powerful than what we thought we were.

> *"Progress is impossible without change, and those who cannot change their minds cannot change anything."*
> — **George Bernard Shaw**

You have the ability, capacity, capability, resources, strength, and wisdom to not only makes changes but to become the change you longed for.

D- Dreams *will create burning desires*

Whatever you can dream of, you can achieve. But you have to put in the effort needed to make them work. What do you want more than anything in the world?

Stop right now and write down your answer.

If you don't know the answer, close your eyes and take time to find the answer. What make you happy? Why?

> *"All our dreams can come true, if we have the courage to pursue them."*
> — **Walt Disney**

You have to prioritise your dreams. Decide on which one is most important to you and focus purely on that. Always take things one step at a time. Make sure you are clear on what you intend to gain from that particular dream of yours, is it success, self-satisfaction or fame. For some of you it may be a combination of all three. You have to write down the reasons why your dreams are important, the "*whys*" that will give you the purpose, passion and power of life. It will wake you up early in the morning and keep you up late at night. When you know the reasons why you are doing it, you will have a burning desire that will drive you to go the extra mile.

> *"My dream is of a place and a time where America will once again be seen as the last best hope of Earth."*
> **– Abraham Lincoln**

You have to spiritually link achieving the goal to your career. Make your products and services your tool to achieving your heart's desires. This will motivate you to take the essential actions to increase your performance to all-star levels. If you have the need and will power, you will create the burning desire to make it happen.

> *"The biggest adventure you can* ever *take is to live the life of your dreams."*
> **– Oprah Winfrey**

Turn your dream into a burning desire by believing that your dream is achievable and you can achieve it. This will boost your self-

confidence and will drive you to success.

E- Education *to become the expert in your field. If you know more, you will do better.*

Education is the key because without that, you get nowhere in life. Situations may be hard, but one of the ways through life is education! So strive and never give up!

> *"Education is the most powerful weapon which you can use to change the world."*
> **–Nelson Mandela**

Education is important aspect in life, not only for our generation, but also for our future generations.

> *"Live as if you were to die tomorrow. Learn as if you were to live forever."*
> **– Mahatma Gandhi**

The key to success is education: The key is held by YOU, and you will be the one who is responsible for opening the door which will lead you to success.

Life is short. Knowledge has no limit. You have to learn more and more to change the world and inspire others.

F- Failure *is your first step towards success. Learn from your mistakes & failures and go on to the next challenge.*

You shouldn't be disheartened by your first fall, but instead learn from it and take in how to handle the situation again in a much easier way!

> **"** *I have not failed. I've just found* 10000 ways that won't work. *Many of life's failures are people who did not realize how close they were to success when they gave up.***"**
> **-Thomas A. Edison**

Getting up requires falling. If a nine-month-old baby gave up trying to walk after his first fall, he would never be able to walk again, simply because he gave up. We can relate this to anything and everything we do or anything we try to do.

> *"It's fine to celebrate success, but it is more important to heed the lessons of failure."*
> **– Bill Gates**

You have to understand that any time you fail at something; you are one step closer to success. Nothing ends in failure, every time you try again, you learn and earn more experience and gain guidance on how to handle next time.

> *"Before success comes in any man's life, he's sure to meet with much temporary defeat and, perhaps some failures. When defeat overtakes a man, the easiest and the most logical thing to do is to quit. That's exactly what the majority of men do."*
> **– Napoleon Hill**

You will face several temporary defeats but you should not quit under any circumstances. If you quit, then you will be the looser. Failure is an opportunity to learn. Think positive and turn your failure into another opportunity for success.

G- <u>Goals</u> *are Dreams with Deadline.*

"Goals are Dreams with a Deadline." In other words, it's fine to dream of owning an island in the Pacific Ocean but what are your chances of ever actually doing it? Dreaming is fun, but goal setting is actually serious business.

Your goals must be realistic, and something you truly believe you can achieve. Your goals must have a deadline by when you want to reach them. Your goals also should be specific with measurable targets. Instead of saying, *"I want to be financially secure,"* specify what you actually want: *"I will sell 50 toys by Christmas."*

For example, if you're an architect constructing an apartment, you would have specific tasks to complete by a certain date. You would complete one step and then move on to the next, with the end goal of finishing the entire building by a certain date. You would dig out the hole for the foundation, and then you would pour the foundation. You would build the frame, and then continue each necessary task until your building is complete. So the main fact to take in is that you should use small goals as a blueprint to achieve your larger goal.

> *"If you want to live a happy life, tie it to a goal,* not to people or things."
> **– Albert Einstein**

Determine what steps you'll have to take to achieve your goals. For example, you're a small business trying to expand by selling a brand new innovative product. The first steps you would take is to do your market research and see whether it would be cost effective.

Write down your goals! Don't keep them in your head! Once you've written them down, share them with your partner, your best friend, or a colleague. Sharing them will help you feel responsible, and you will have the desire and willpower to work harder to reach your goals. You have to remember that your goals are not written in stone. You have to set goals to start. As time passes and you gain more experience and learn more about your business, you can always modify your goals, mainly your long-term ones.

In order to accomplish your goals, you may have to acquire some new skills and step out of your comfort zone. You must be willing to do whatever it takes! Change is not something you should be afraid of; it's the one thing that you should face head on.

> *"You can only become truly accomplished at something you love. Don't make money your goal. Instead, pursue the things you love doing, and then do them so well that people can't take their eyes off you."*
> **– Maya Angelou**

Never give up! If you are determined to succeed, and if you KNOW that you can, nothing can stop you!

H- History - *learn from the histories of world leaders.*

History is filled with the achievements of great leaders. By examining the past we can retain key attributes that will help us succeed to where we want to be.

> *"There are so many people who have lived and died before you. You will never have a new problem; you're not going to ever have a new problem. Somebody wrote the answer down in a book somewhere."*
> **– Will Smith**

So what were the great leaders so good at, and how did they achieve the things that made them great?

The short answer is that they weren't all good at everything, but quite the contrary. Each leader had their own strengths and weaknesses which drove them to where they are today, as an individual who's looked up upon by others as a great achiever. Many were so brilliant at certain things that it hid the fact that they were indifferent at others.

When it comes to improving our skills, history's great leaders provide lessons for us. So learn from the leaders.

I-Innovation for continuous Improvement

You have to innovate continuously to be a market leader. BlackBerry missed the innovation part and Apple used continuous innovation techniques to dominate the market.

The economic recession had the effect of encouraging us to focus on what we are going to lose, rather than what we have to gain. If you don't take any risk, there won't be any return or innovation or growth. You have to be proactive and show others how forward thinking innovative ideas could save a fortune.

Six Steps Guide for Innovation

1. Question everything with **WHY** to seek deeper.

2. Always **CARE** for your people you are trying to serve. This will help you to find the better way to serve your customer in an innovative way. This will help you to practice continuous innovation, which will bring you more success.

3. Networking and **CONNECTING** with others to bring different concepts in a new, exciting and innovative way.

4. **ENCOURAGE** everyone to think outside of the box to come up with new ideas.

5. **TEST** new ideas right away to find out whether you've touched on something truly promising

6. Get **FEEDBACK** from other people to innovate your product or service.

J- Jealousy is the Silent Killer

If you are truly comfortable and secure with yourselves, jealousy can't get in your way. Look within, spend time with yourself, get to know the real you. Choose to focus on yourself, instead of the person you are jealous of. Use your understanding of desires and your mind to change your perception. Know that you have everything you need to be whole, happy and complete right inside of you. Know that if you feel something is missing that you can have it, you can achieve it.

Six Steps Guide to Overcome Jealousy

1. Love yourself. You are very important in this world
2. Focus on your strengths and abilities
3. Stop comparing yourself against others
4. Just focus on what you want in your life
5. Build your self-confidence
6. Shift your focus to positive thoughts

K- Knowledge is Power

You have to be ready to gain adequate knowledge and skill to perform your task. You should not rely on other people.

> *"An investment in knowledge pays the best interest."*
> **– Benjamin Franklin**

You have to invest in yourself to gain more knowledge.
You have to empower your employees to gain more knowledge. This will encourage and motivate them to come up with new innovative ideas.

L- Leadership for Empowerment

Leaders think and talk about solutions. Followers think and talk about problems. You have to be a good leader to become very successful.

> *"As we look ahead into the next century, leaders will be those who empower others."*
> **– Bill Gates**
>
> *"It is better to lead from behind and to put others in front, especially when you celebrate victory when nice things occur. You take the front line when there is danger. Then people will appreciate your leadership."*
> **– Nelson Mandela**

You have to work with your employees and show them how to perform the task rather than just tell them and then blame them for the mistakes. You have to give clear instructions and timely guidance. You have to lead by example. When success comes you have to pass the rewards to your employees and when you face defeat you have to take in-charge and motive your employees to turn the defeat into victory. You have to create a vision into each of your employees by combining your company vision with their dreams. This will create the most powerful and highly motivated employees, who will bring success to you.

M- Mind Power for Creativity

Your brain is a muscle. You need to exercise it regularly. You have to invest some time to regularly train your brain to increase its power.

You have to try new things. This creates new neural pathways, increasing your intelligence. Go to the gym or do general exercise. Regular exercise helps to increase brain function and enhances neurogenesis. You have to feed your brain with a healthy diet (i.e. fresh fruit and vegetables). Our diets have a big impact on brain function. You have to train yourself into logical thinking. By questioning everything, this will force your brain to innovate and create new ideas. All of these will help you to get enough sleep.

Reading would help to trigger your imagination, which relieves tension and stress. You have to develop positive thinking. This will help you to go from negative to positive thinking which will activate the subconscious mind that will drive you to success.

N- Niche Market to Focus

Your niche is the service you specialise in offering to your target market. Niche marketing will help you to focus on a specific group of people, and what their specific needs and wants are. **You can easily identify specific clients in your Niche market.**

Six Steps Guide to Your Niche Market

1. You have to become an expert and well known in your niche.
2. You have to build the trust with more visibility and credibility, which will bring more clients to you.
3. You have to create and provide customised service, based on your client needs. This will help you to retain your clients.
4. You have to innovate and extend your services to keep your customers happy.
5. You have to build your network within your niche to improve your brand.
6. You have to remember that happy customers will bring more customers to you.

O- <u>Opportunities</u> around You

You have to be an open-minded person to spot opportunities around you.

> *"If there is a God, he is within. You don't ask God to give you things; you depend on God for your inner theme."*
> **– Bruce Lee**

A story of opportunities:

In a small village lived a man who spent his entire life serving God. One day heavy rain and flooding started. The whole village was filled with water which was slowly deepening. That man stayed in his place and prayed to God to save him. A boat went by with lots of people on board. A woman cried out to the man to come aboard, however, the man replied that the God which he prayed to would save him. Finally as the water deepened up to his shoulders, a log floated by for him to hold on to and survive, however, he was determined that his God would save him. Eventually he drowned. When he reached heaven, he asked God, "I served my entire life for you, why did you not save me?" God then replied, "I did, my son. I gave you so many opportunities. I was the one on the boat who cried for you to come aboard and I was the floating log urging you to grab hold. It was you who missed all those opportunities given to you and now you blame me for your mistakes."

> *"To hell with circumstances; I create opportunities."*
> **– Bruce Lee**

Now what the story is merely telling us is that you create your own opportunities; don't rely on others to get you there.

P- Persistence with Patience

Persistence is the ability to stick with something. The majority of people face failure because of their lack of persistence in creating alternative plans to take the place of those which fail.

> *"Patience, persistence and perspiration make an unbeatable combination for success"*
> **– Napoleon Hill**

Six Steps guide to improve your Persistence

1. You have to write down your purpose
2. You have to create a burning desire within yourself
3. You have to create will power
4. You have to stop acting on guesses
5. You have to gain accurate knowledge
6. You have to overcome all of your fears

Q- Quality is your Brand

You have to make sure that you provide service of quality to your customers.

> *"There is one quality which one must possess to win, and that is definiteness of purpose, the knowledge of what one wants, and a burning desire to possess it."*
> **– Napoleon Hill**

Six Steps Guide to Achieve Quality

1. Define your purpose
2. Gain knowledge of what you want
3. Identify your strengths and weaknesses
4. Create a burning desire
5. Listen, learn and understand your customers
6. Focus on continuous improvement

R- Results at the end is Key

You have to be results oriented; nothing else. As a leader you have to be very proactive; to inspire others to perform at their best and always think ahead with the goal of avoiding problems before they arise. You have to be in charge, and take responsibility and take initiative. You should not blame others for any of your wrong actions.

Six Steps Guide to Achieve Your Result

1. Define your target
2. Set measurement for performance
3. Analyse the variance and take on time action
4. Improve your profit
5. Control your cost
6. Study your competitors for better results

S- Sacrifice for Success

If you want to achieve something in your life for the long-term benefit, you have to sacrifice something in short term. For example, if you are attending a training program, you have to cut some play time.

You have to list your priorities and think in advance whether you are ready to sacrifice. You can use the delegation to achieve success with less sacrifice.

T- Time is more important than Money

> *"Time is our most valuable asset, yet we tend to waste it, kill it, and spend it rather than invest it."*
> **– Jim Rohn**

Most people leave home at 8 am for work and come back at 6 pm, then dinner, TV, Facebook and so on. So you do not have the time to think of something else which could bring more fortune in the future. This has to be changed. You have to prioritise your tasks and keep yourself free to develop yourself towards success. You have to invest your time to learn new skills, try new opportunities and inspire others.

As is always said, *"time is precious"*; it's something that cannot be retrieved, so make the most of it.

Six Steps Guide to Improve Your Time Management Skills

1. Make a list
2. Prioritise and do the important task first
3. Reward yourself for accomplishment of a task
4. Focus on one thing at a time
5. Avoid procrastination
6. Set a deadline and monitor your progress

U- Understand Before You Start

You have to understand your customers' needs and wants rather than thinking about your own benefits. Then you can think the way of providing customised service in your niche market.

Six Must Understand Things Before You Start Your Business

1. Understanding of compliance such as licensing, registration, laws, etc.
2. Understanding the scope of your business such as size of the company initially and how you plan to expand in the future, and what type of services or products you can offer
3. Marketing, identifying your target audience and how to best reach them
4. Financing and space requirements of your business
5. Understand your competitors and how you plan to build your business and reach your business goals
6. Forms of support needed to start and run your business

V- Vision for Success

You have to have the vision to drive yourself quickly towards success. You have to visualise every single day that you have already reached that level and enjoy that feeling. This will power your mind and will create the burning desire towards success.

> *"If you are working on something exciting that you really care about, you don't have to be pushed. The vision pulls you."*
> **— Steve Jobs**

You can go back to Chapter 6, The Powerful Formula for Success and refer to THE POWER OF VISION to learn more about Vision.

W- Win-Win for Long Term Relationships

Whether you are negotiating with your supplier or employee or anyone who could contribute to your long-term relationship and business success, you have to reach a Win-Win situation.

Six Steps Guide for Win-Win Situation
1. Listen carefully and show interest in the other party
2. Be open minded and flexible during your communication
3. Offer more than one solution to the problem
4. Know what you want out of negotiation and what the other party thinks he or she wants
5. Know your best alternative and the other party's best alternative
6. Be patient and prepare for worst case scenarios and best case scenarios

X- X-Efficiency for Lowest Cost

This concept introduced by economist Harvey Liebenstein. You have to use your workers, machines, technology, etc., to produce maximum output at the lowest cost and as quickly as possible.

Y- You are the Most Valuable Asset

Treat yourself like a king and always think that you are the most important and powerful person on the planet. You are the only one person who can control yourself.

Z- Zero based budgeting for efficient resource allocation

This budgeting technique is established on needs and benefits rather than history. You have to identify your task first. Then focus on funding resources to complete the task. You will do this by selecting the cheapest way to finish each and every task. It's the most efficient allocation of your resources.

DREAM BIG
ACTION PLANNER

TASK 1

List 6 opportunities that are available to you

1.

2.

3.

4.

5.

6.

Now think of 6 ways of how you will use these opportunities to your advantage.

....

....

....

....

....

....

....

....

....

TASK 2

List 6 tasks you will undertake each week to increase your mind power through spiritual energy and healthy lifestyle.

1.

2.

3.

4.

5.

6.

What is your action plans to overcome your fears.

....

....

....

....

....

....

....

....

....

....

....

....

....

TASK 3

List 6 lessons you have learned from our inspirational leaders.

1.

2.

3.

4.

5.

6.

Now write down your dream that you have most yearned to achieve. Start visualising you are already living in that world, mainly when you wake up every morning and before you go to bed.

....
....
....
....
....
....
....
....
....
....
....
....

TASK 4

List 6 ways to overcome your procrastinating factors.

1.

2.

3.

4.

5.

6.

List 6 ways in which you will turn your defeats into victory.

1.

2.

3.

4.

5.

6.

TASK 5

List 6 action plans to build your positive thinking.

1.

2.

3.

4.

5.

6.

Use the *A to Z SUCCESS MODEL* ™ to start your journey towards your final destination.

TASK 6

Brainstorm your ideas and start implementing them into your day to day life! Start NOW!

BRAINSTORM YOUR IDEAS:

BRAINSTORM YOUR IDEAS:

~CHAPTER 12~

HOW TO ANSWER INTERVIEW QUESTIONS

1. Can you tell me a little about yourself?

Don't give your complete employment or personal history. Instead just give a pitch saying exactly why you're the right fit for the job. Start off with the 2-3 specific accomplishments or experiences that you most want the interviewer to know about, and then wrap up talking about how that prior experience has placed you for this specific role.

2. How did you hear about the position?

This is actually a perfect opportunity to stand out and show your passion for and connection to the company. For example, if you found out about this job through a friend or professional contact, name drop that person, then share why you were so excited about it, specifically, caught your eye about the role.

3. What do you know about the company?

Try to show them you care about it the company mission and goals.

4. Why do you want this job?

Companies want to hire people who are passionate about the job, so you should have a great answer about why you want the position. Identify the key factors that make the role a great fit for you. For example "I think you guys are doing great on customer service and business expansion, so I want to be a part of it"

5. Why should we hire you?

Sell yourself and your skills to the hiring manager. You can not only do the work, you can deliver great results. You'll really fit in with the team and culture and that you'd be a better hire than any of the other candidates.

6. What are your greatest professional strengths?

Share your true strengths that are most targeted to this particular position.

7. What do you consider to be your weaknesses?

Objective is to identify your self-awareness and honesty. Say something that you struggle with but that you're working to improve. For example, maybe you've never been strong at public speaking, but you've recently volunteered to run meetings to help you be more comfortable when addressing a crowd.

8. What is your greatest professional achievement?

Nothing says "hire me" better than a track record of achieving amazing results in past jobs, so don't be shy when answering this question! A great way to do so is by using the S-T-A-R method:

Set up the situation

Task that you were required to complete

Action you have taken

Result archived.

9. Tell me about a challenge or conflict you've faced at work, and how you dealt with it.

Objective is to find out how you will respond to conflict.

Use S-T-A-R method, being sure to focus on how you handled the situation professionally and productively, and ideally closing with a happy ending, like how you came to a resolution or compromise.

10. Where do you see yourself in five years?

Objective of this question is to find out whether you have set realistic expectations for your career and also to find out whether you have ambition which aligns with your goals and growth

11. What's your dream job?

Interviewer wants to uncover whether this position is really in line with your ultimate career goals. Talk about your goals and ambitions and why this job will get you closer to them.

12. What other companies are you interviewing with?

Objective is to find out what the competition is for you? And also to find out whether you're serious about the industry

13. Why are you leaving your current job?

Keep things positive. You have nothing to gain by being negative about your past employers. Shows that you're eager to take on new opportunities and that the role you're interviewing for is a better fit for you than your current or last position. For example, "I'd really love to be part of blue chip senior management team and I know I'd have that opportunity here." If you can position the learning experience as an advantage for this next job, even better.

14. What are you looking for in a new position? What

type of work environment do you prefer?

Be specific. List same things that this position has to offer Mention similar to the environment of the company you're applying to.

15. What were your bosses' strengths/weaknesses?

They want to see how you handle tough questions.

They want to hear something positive

They want to know your weakness won't affect your performance.

16. What's your management style?

The best managers are strong but flexible; I tend to approach my employee relationships as a coach. Share a couple of your best managerial moments, like when you grew your team from 2 to 10 or coached an underperforming employee to become the company's top salesperson.

17. What's a time you exercised leadership?

Choose an example that showcases your project management skills and ability to confidently and effectively lead a team.

18. What's a time you disagreed with a decision that was made at work?

Objective is to find our whether you can do so in a productive, professional way. Tell the one where your actions made a positive difference on the outcome of the situation, whether it was a work-related outcome or a more effective and productive working relationship.

19. How would your boss and co-workers describe you?

Tell about your strength, your strong work ethic or your willingness to work in on any projects when needed.

20. If you have a gap in your employment

I decided to take a break at the time for impressive volunteer/ blogging or taking classes but today I'm ready to contribute to this organization in the following ways."

21. If you have changed career paths

Give a few examples of how your past experience is transferrable to the new role.

22. How do you deal with pressure or stressful situations?

Choose an answer that shows that you can meet a stressful situation head-on in a productive, positive manner and let nothing stop you from accomplishing your goal. By making to-do list

23. What would your first 30, 60, or 90 days look like in this role?

What you'd need to do to get ramped up.

What information would you need?

What parts of the company would you need to familiarize yourself with?

What other employees would you want to sit down with?

Choose a couple of areas where you think you can make meaningful contributions right away.

24. What are your salary requirements?

State the highest number in that range that applies based on your experience, education, and skills. Then tell you want the job and are willing to negotiate.

25. What do you like to do outside of work?

Objective is to see whether you will fit in with the culture and gives you the opportunity to open up and display their personality too.

26. Who are our competitors? What do you think we could do better or differently?

Please carry out enough research about the company. Whether you have some background on the company and you're able to think critically about it and come to the table with new ideas. How could the company increase profit/ improve customer service.

27. What motivates you?

If you're someone that loves a challenge, then maybe mentioning that you're at your most motivated when faced with unforeseen or even expected challenges and overcoming them would be a good idea.

If you're interviewing for a Social Media Manager role, you could say that helping customers and engaging with fans motivates you to do your best every day), but there are certain answers you can give which apply to any job, however these should be customised to the position you're interviewing for.

For example, if you thrive on coming up with new ways of approaching tasks or projects, then saying that being innovative and finding new, more effective ways of working motivates you would be a good answer.

28. What's your availability?

- Don't leave your current job without sufficient notice to your employer.

- Don't give notice to your current employer until you are holding a written job offer – that you have accepted, preferably in writing – in your hands.

29. Would you work 40+ hours a week?

Objective is to find out whether you got time management skills to finish the task on time and also whther you can work more hours if needed. i.e some urgent tasks with tight deadline

30. Do you have any questions for us?

It's your opportunity to sniff out whether a job is the right fit for you. What do you want to know about the position? The company? The department? The team? What can you tell me about your new products or plans for growth?

~CHAPTER 13~

CV WRITING TIPS

1) Identify what qualifies you for the role

2) Select a simple and standardized format, don't go for anything too fancy.

3) Please double check and make sure your contact information is accurate and up-to-date with a primary contact number, a mobile phone number and email address. Put your name and contact details at the top of the page, then use the job title itself as a heading. Under this, summarise key details such experience in a particular skill, project experience or a short branding statement highlighting your strengths and attributes. Include a brief cover letter explaining your reasons for applying, and interest in the company.

4) Include an objective statement to tell the employer about your strongest and most desirable personality is applicable to the job you are applying for.

5) If you have no work experience, not to worry. List your volunteer work or community activities or work experience through a course at school or course work at school that you feel is relevant to the job, career oriented education and any academic achievements or awards. Explain how you think your excellent performance in these areas would benefit the

employer and enhance your ability to do the job. Try to get a letter of reference from a teacher of one of the courses you mention.

6) Think from the employer's perspective. Decide on the most interesting factors, where you have used relevant skills, and then make these prominent on your CV. Voluntary or community involvement, work placements, coursework, personal projects and extracurricular activities can all be highlighted to show your suitability.

7) Think of any project that you undertook at School or University or Personal, which is relevant to this job. Break down your projects into target, result and learned competencies to shows relevant skills, achievements, ability to get on with others, organisational and communication skills.

8) Quantify your achievements where possible such as how much money saved, percentage of time reduced, etc

9) Try to use keywords such as decision making, risk management, etc under skills and work experience section.

10) If you have a position of authority in any of the groups make note of it and describe your duties.

11) **List any awards you've received or the subjects you've excelled at in school.** Awards are not easy to get, thus they show commitment and hard work.

12) Use action-oriented words to describe responsibilities.

- Innovated
- Motivated
- Facilitated

- Organized
- Managed

13) Please make the most of your qualities such as your skills, attitude, potential and enthusiasm.

14) Don't lie and always be true to who you are.

15) Make yourself look good. It's not lying.

For example, if you were the person at your previous job to clean up the mess at the end of the day, you might say that as follows:

"I have facilitated teamwork by organizing the work site more efficiently". This is not lying.

16) Sell yourself by making a list of your skills, special talents, or positive personality traits.

17) When writing your first resume don't make it more than a page. Employers will not expect a long work history from a first time worker.

18) Put the most important information first. You don't need to always use a strict chronological work history format. Relevant project work can come before less relevant employment.

19) Find great references.

Your teacher or previous employer or adviser can also be great references. Only pick contacts who will say good things about you.

20) Talk to your contacts in advance and coach them slightly

on the nature of the job and what you are applying for.

~CHAPTER 14~

IT'S NOT WHO YOU KNOW BUT WHO KNOWS YOU?

TOP 10 BENEFITS OF NETWORKING:

1) Opens the Door to Connect and Talk to Highly Influential People.

Reaching highly influenced individuals is very difficult in normal conditions.

"It's not WHAT you know, but WHO you know"

2) Increases the Chance of Getting Suitable Jobs

In current economic climate, job market is very competitive. Therefore highly influential connections would increase the chances of referrals for jobs.

3) Your Confidence Level Will Increase

Regular networking would help you to push yourself to talk to people you don't know and you will get increased confidence the more you do this.

4) Positive Influence and Positive Energy

It is important to be surrounding yourself with positive, uplifting people that help you to grow. The people that you hang around with and talk to do influence who you are and what you do.

5) New Opportunities will Come to You

Opportunities within networking are really endless such as joint ventures, clients, business partnerships, speaking, writing opportunities and so on. You should not jump into all opportunities. Have a vision and set goals. Then use networking to find the right opportunities.

6) Improved Decision Making

If you want to be really successful, then you need to have a great source of relevant connections in your network that you can call when needed to make the right decision.

7) Raising Your Profile and Reputation

Build your reputation as a knowledgeable, reliable and supportive person by offering useful information or tips to people. Being visible and getting noticed is a big benefit of networking.

8) Knowledge Sharing

Networking is great for sharing ideas and knowledge and allows you to see things from another perspective. Whether it's asking for feedback or discussing your point of view, it will help you expand your knowledge and would help to avoid making the same mistakes again. This will save lots of time and money.

9) Develop Your Skills

Networking would increase your communication, presentation, time management, team working, leadership and problem solving skills by talking with lots of new people in different areas.

10) Personal Satisfaction of Helping Others

Everyone has their own problems. And all problems can be solved. Networking would give an opportunity to help other people to solve their problems. You should not expect anything in return for the advice. For each and every help you do you will automatically get the return in some form. Personal satisfaction of helping others is the biggest return.

~CHAPTER 15~

HOW TO USE LINKEDIN TO BUILD YOUR PROFESSIONAL BRAND

1) Your photo

LinkedIn profile picture should be a professional photo

2) Your headline

Try to stand out by stating what you have to offer and identifying your unique selling point to attract recruiters.

Examples:

DO: Accounting Graduate, Specialising in management Accounting.

Interested in strategic decision making

DON'T: Motivated Graduate Looking to Work in

Accounting

3) Your summary

You should focus on what you want to do and include achievements to attract a lot of eyeballs. You could upload a short video clip where you talk about yourself.

4) Your keywords

The more industry-relevant keywords you have in your profile, the higher you are on a recruiter's search rankings. This increases the chances of your profile getting noticed.

5) Your education section

This is an important networking tool, which would help you to connect with your alumni.

6) Claim your vanity URL

Personalise the web address for your LinkedIn profile this would help you appear on Google, if employers search for you

7) Your public profile settings:

Go to your public profile and set visible on your public profile. I would recommend having the summary, your current position, skills and education visible.

8) Your connections

Connecting with all students would help to find out how other college graduates found a job or got hired by an employer.

You can import your email list to find out who among your friends is present on LinkedIn.

You also can connect with people outside of your network. You can do an introduction through a common connection

9) Join Groups

By joining the larger groups, with the most number of members, you can increase your potential network. Take part in group discussions. You can even start discussions asking for advice related to your job search, such as recommendations for good courses, training and vacancies.

10) Get Recommendations

If you have more recommendations, you will have a great chance of attracting the employers' attention.

11) Set Job Alerts

Helpful for you to receive notifications of recommended jobs. Employers post vacancies with the hope of jobseeker like you will come across them and turn out to be the ideal candidate.

12) Post status update daily

This will increase your visibility. If you do have a Twitter account, you can integrate into your LinkedIn account to get more audience.

13) Use applications to reach more audience

SlideShare to share presentations of your company or about specials or promotions you have on at the moment,

Google Docs to get video going on your profile

Blog Link application for bloggers

This would attract employer's attention and increase the chances of a company inviting you for an interview or referral from other professionals.

14) Find suitable events to attend

You can find the relevant events on LinkedIn by using key words search. This would help you meet professionals in person would open new opportunities.

LinkedIn would help you to get largest connection of global professional network, improved personal brand, improved recognition, improved visibility, new opportunities, etc.

ECONOMY COLLAPSE

MARKET CRASH

WHERE TO INVEST?

INVEST IN YOU!

ABOUT THE AUTHOR

Mayooran lives in England with his lovely wife and two adorable children.

Mayooran started his career with KPMG in 2006 and is currently working as Group Finance Director in London, where he is managing £50 Million turnover businesses with over 1000 employees.

Mayooran is currently reading his DOCTORATE degree in Business Administration at Edinburgh Business School, Heriot-Watt University. He is also a Chartered Global Management Accountant (ACMA, UK), holding an MSc Degree in Accounting with Finance and a BSc degree in Mathematics.

Mayooran is an award winning author and amazon No 1 best seller. He helps people to write and publish their books in 30 days. Mayooran has published his own online course, that currently has more than 5000 students.

This book reflects his experience gained by learning from world class leaders, teaching students, mentoring undergraduates and also by working for global giants and small businesses. This book will completely change the way you view your thinking. As an Award Winning Author and International Bestseller, **Mayooran** encourages you to show what is really possible, rather than let you become victims of an economy in crisis. This book will open your eyes to some of the completely new, different and exciting opportunities which are now available for you.

Mayooran works with students to address the vital issues affecting their education and to inspire them to be future leaders. He works in the corporate world and gives back through coaching orphanages around the world, to give both children and adults hope for a brighter tomorrow.

You can contact **Mayooran** on:
www.dvgstar.co.uk
www.dvgstar.com
www.universallearningacademy.com

Facebook: www.facebook.com/mayooran.senthilmani
LinkedIn: www.linkedin.com/in/mayooransenthilmani

MAYOORAN'S PUBLICATIONS

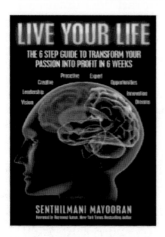

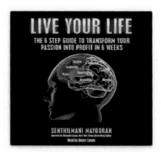

AUDIO BOOK

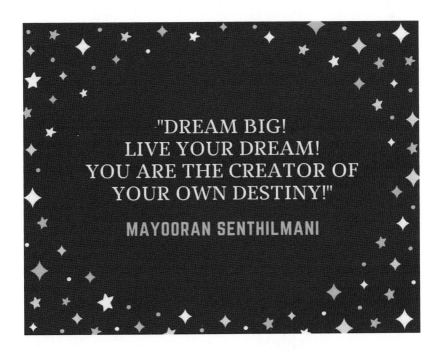

REFERENCES & BIBLIOGRAPHY

1) Eurydice network, March 2012
(http://eacea.ec.europa.eu/education/eurydice)

2) Daniel Priestley, Entrepreneur Revolution: How to
Develop Your Entrepreneurial Mindset and Start a
Business That Works, March 2013.

3) Napoleon Hill, Think And Grow Rich , 30 Apr 2010
4) Raymond Aaron, Double Your Income Doing What
You Love: Raymond Aaron's Guide to Power Mentoring,
Jan 2008)
5) http://www.spiritualresearchfoundation.org

6) http://www.ourspiritatwork.com

http://www.theatlantic.com/magazine/archive/2013/11/
innovations-list/309536/